The Thinking TREE

www.DyslexiaGames.com

Dyslexia Games Series B –Book 6
Friendly Copyright Notice:

The Thinking Tree LLC ● 617 N Swope St. ● Greenfield, IN 46140 ● info@dyslexiagames.com ● **+1 317-622-8852**

Animal Talk

Sweet & Silly Animal Poems, Drawing Games & Spelling Lessons.

By Sarah J. Brown

Parent Teacher Instructions:

Provide the student with a pencil, eraser, a set of sharp colored pencils, and a fine point black pen.

This workbook requires the teacher to spend a few minutes reading with the child. Before your student begins each lesson read the short poem at the top of the page to the child while he or she listens. Then read it again and have the child repeat each line back to you. Read the poem a third time together. Next see if he or she can read it alone, or repeat it from memory while pointing to each word. The child does not have to read perfectly to complete the lesson, this is a learning exercise, not a test. The goal is to look for clues to find the word that is missing and write it in the blank box. As the lessons progress they become more challenging.

These exercises develop tracking skills, memory skills, teach word recognition and spelling while tapping into the creative area of the child's mind. Be sure to talk about the animals in each poem.

Give the child time to add color to the animals on each page.

Fill in the missing words:

I found a turtle by the <u>pond</u> <u>and</u> named him Mr. Green.
I let him <u>taste</u> my ice cream cone, and <u>gave</u> him all my <u>beans</u>.

I found a turtle by the _____

_____ named him Mr. Green.

I let him _____ my ice cream cone,

and _____ him all my _____

pond   and   taste   gave   beans

Name:_____   Date:_____

Little kitten, play with <u>me</u>. <u>Here</u> is a catnip mouse.
Little kitten, chase my <u>string</u> all <u>over</u> the <u>house</u>.

Little kitten, play with

_____ is a catnip mouse.

Little kitten, chase my _____ ,

All _____ the _____ .

me   Here   string   over   house

Name:_____   **Date:**_____

Puppy dog, puppy <u>dog</u>, are you <u>lost</u> and alone?
You chased a <u>pretty</u> butterfly, puppy <u>please</u> come <u>home</u>.

Puppy dog, puppy ___ .

Are you ___ and alone?

You chased a ___ butterfly,

puppy ___ come ___ .

dog   lost   pretty   please   home

Name:_____   **Date:**_____

Mary had a little <u>lamb</u>, I'd <u>like</u> to have one too.
When I <u>grow</u> up I want to own a <u>pet shop</u>, farm or zoo.

Mary had a little _____

I'd _____ to have one too.

When I _____ up

I want to own a _____ , farm or _____ .

lamb   like   grow   Pet shop   zoo

Little squirrel, I'm like <u>you</u>, I <u>love</u> to climb the trees.
<u>Little</u> squirrel, be my friend, we'll play with nuts and <u>leaves</u>.

Little squirrel, I'm like  ,
I ___ to climb the trees.
___ squirrel, be my friend,
we'll ___ with nuts and ___ .

you   love   Little   play   leaves

Name:_____   **Date:**_____

Snails and <u>slugs</u> are grey and brown, sometimes they are <u>green</u>. <u>Snails</u> and slugs make <u>good</u> pets if you like <u>slimy</u> things.

Snails and  are grey and brown,

sometimes they are 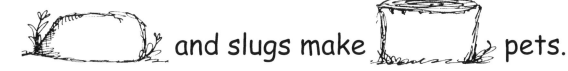.

 and slugs make  pets.

if  like  things.

Name:_____ **Date:**_____

Sometimes I chase <u>the</u> rooster, sometimes he <u>chases</u> me.
<u>But</u> I can never catch <u>him</u>, unless he's fast <u>asleep</u>.

Sometimes I chase _____ rooster,

sometimes he _____ me.

_____ I can never catch _____ ,

unless he's fast _____ .

Name:_____ **Date:**_____

I'd like to catch <u>that</u> rabbit, but he's too <u>fast</u> for me.
So I <u>will</u> build a <u>rabbit</u> house with <u>carrots</u> and green leaves.

I'd like to catch ⬚ rabbit,

but he's too ⬚ for me.

So I ⬚ build a ⬚ house

with ⬚ and green leaves.

Name:_____ **Date:**_____

I'm building you a <u>bird</u> house and <u>filling</u> it with seeds.
I'll <u>paint</u> it blue and <u>purple</u> and hang it in a <u>tree</u>.

I'm building you a ⬜ house

and ⬜ it with seeds.

I'll ⬜ it blue and ⬜ ,

and hang it in a ⬜ .

Name:_____ **Date:**_____

Butterfly, butterfly, my garden's in bloom
My flowers are waiting, I hope you come soon!

Butterfly, [_____],

my [_____] in bloom

My [_____] are waiting,

I hope [_____] you

Name:_____ **Date:**_____

Spring is here and birds appear . In every tree they sing.
It's my favorite time of year when winter turns to spring!

Spring is here and _____ appear.

In every _____ they sing.

It's my favorite _____ of year

when _____ turns to spring!

Name:_____ **Date:**_____

Little piggy, here I come with something just for you!
I saved my crusts and apple cores, and carrots from my stew!

Little , here I come

with something for you!

I saved my crusts and cores,

and from my stew!

Name:_____ **Date:**_____

I'd like to have a dozen goats, I'd be happy with just one.
I'd teach it tricks, and brush its coat, and take it for a run.

I'd like to have a 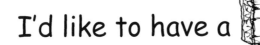 goats,

I'd be  with just one.

I'd teach it tricks, and  it's coat,

and  it for a run.

Use a black pen
to draw the missing horn:

Name:_____   **Date:**_____

I had a baby bunny that did not like his cage.
So I put him in the garden, much to Mom's dismay!

I had a  bunny

that did like his cage.

So I put him in the ,

much to dismay!

Use a black pen
to draw the missing eye:

Name:_____ **Date:**_____

A mouse was in my garden eating beans and kale.
When kitty came to catch him, he hid beneath a pail.

A mouse was in my ,

eating  and kale.

When  came to catch him,

he hid beneath a .

Use a black pen
to draw the missing paw:

Name:_____ **Date:**_____

My best friend is a friendly duck. He thinks that I'm his mother!
He follows me around the yard. We have so much fun together.

My best  is a friendly duck.

He _____ that I'm his mother!

He _____ me around the yard

We have so _____ fun together.

Use a black pen
to draw the missing beak:

Name:_____ Date:_____

There is a special time of year, but I don't remember when.
The ladybugs sneak in my house. I don't know how they get in!

There is a special  of year,

but I don't remember  .

The ladybugs  in my house.

I don't 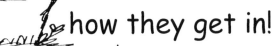 how they get in!

Use a black pen
to draw the missing part:

Name:_____ **Date:**_____

I would like to train a tiger, if I worked at the zoo.

I would teach him to play baseball, and how to tie a shoe.

I would like to ⬚ a tiger,

if I worked at the ⬚ .

I would ⬚ him to play baseball,

and how to ⬚ a shoe.

Use a black pen
to draw the missing ear:

Name:_____ Date:_____

Once I found a tree frog, we both were climbing trees.
I watched him climb the branches and hide among the leaves.

Once I found a tree ,

we  were climbing trees.

I watched him  the branches

and hide among the

Use a black pen
to draw the missing eye:

Name:_____ Date:_____

Bees are fun to watch, but stay far from the hive!
I once learned this the hard way, and I'm glad to be alive!

Bees are  to watch,

but ____ far from the hive!

I once learned ____ the hard way,

and I'm glad to be ____ !

Use a black pen
to draw the
missing wing:

Somewhere along the trail, far from the busy road.
I heard a creature croaking, it must have been a toad.

Somewhere  the trail,

far from the busy  .

I  a creature croaking,

it must have been a  .

Use a black pen
to draw the missing mouth:

Name:_____   **Date:**_____

I'll be riding on a fine horse, when I am twenty-four.
I've saved up fifty dollars, but mom says I'll need lots more.

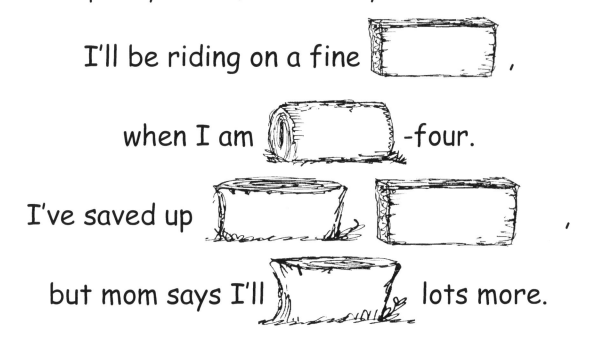

I'll be riding on a fine [   ] ,

when I am [   ] -four.

I've saved up [   ] [   ] ,

but mom says I'll [   ] lots more.

Use a black pen
to draw the missing reigns:

Name:_____ **Date:**_____

Dogs are fun to play with. They run and catch the ball.
Dogs will give big kisses and come each time we call.

Dogs are fun to [   ] with.

They run and [   ] the ball.

Dogs will [   ] big kisses

and come [   ] time we call.

Use a black pen
to draw the missing nose:

Name:_____ Date:_____

Hens and chicks are silly. Have you ever watched them play?
The chicks are soft and fluffy and the hens have much to say.

Hens and ⬚ are silly.

Have you ever watched ⬚ play?

The chicks are ⬚ and fluffy

and the hens ⬚ much to say.

Use a black pen
to draw the missing chick:

Name:_____ **Date:**_____

I will sit here in the forest, I will be still for half a day.
The rabbits don't know that I'm here, and I like it this way.

I will sit 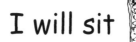 in the forest,

I will be still for  a day.

The rabbits don't  that I'm here,

and I  it this way.

Use a black pen
to draw the missing ear:

Name:_____ **Date:**_____

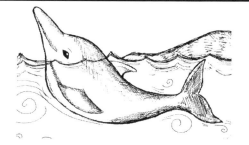

Listen to my dolphin sing. Watch her dance and play.
When the sun is going down she splashes in its rays.

Listen to my  sing.

Watch her _____ and play.

When the sun is _____ down

she _____ in it's rays.

Use a black pen
to draw the missing fin:

Name:_____ **Date:**_____

Goldfish are such lovely pets. They never bark or bite.
They swim and play all through the day, and never pick a fight.

Goldfish are such  pets.

They never  or bite.

They swim and play all  the day,

and never pick a  .

Use a black pen
to draw the missing fish:

Name:_____ Date:_____

I'm as happy as a bear cub playing with his mom.
I'm as sleepy as a brown bear, napping all day long.

I'm as happy as a [_____] cub

playing [_____] his mom.

I'm as sleepy as a [_____] bear,

napping all day [_____].

Use a black pen
to draw the missing face:

Two baby seals jump and play, they seem to smile too.

Do you like to watch the seals splashing at the zoo?

Two baby [ ] jump and play,

they seem to [ ] too.

Do you like to [ ] the seals

[ ] at the zoo?

Use a black pen
to draw the missing eye:

Name:_____   **Date:**_____

If I were a tree frog I'd climb the highest tree.
I'd sit up there all summer, or until my mom called me.

If I [ ] a tree frog

I'd climb the [ ] tree.

I'd sit up [ ] all summer,

or [ ] my mom called me.

Use a black pen
to draw the missing leaves:

Name:_____ **Date:**_____

If I had a guinea pig I'd name her "Bonnie Blue".

I'd give her my umbrella and my nicest pair of shoes.

If I had a [ ] pig

I'd [ ] her "Bonnie Blue".

I'd give her my [ ]

And [ ] her in Dad's shoe.

Use a black pen
to draw the missing eyes:

Name:_____   Date:_____

My momma had a donkey. That donkey was not good.

My momma had to chase it all through the neighborhood.

My momma had a .

That donkey  not good.

My momma had to  it

all  the neighborhood.

Use a black pen
to draw the missing ear:

Name:_____ **Date:_____**

Animal Talk

Certificate of Completion

_____

Name & Age

_____

Date of Completion

The Thinking
TREE

_____

Dyslexia Games

_____

Teacher

The Thinking
TREE

www.DyslexiaGames.com

Created by: Sarah Janisse Brown